I0803688

Five-Finger Positions Rule!

Seven Mid-Elementary Piano Solos
by
Carolyn Miller

Contents

12143

Country Garden

Moderato

Carolyn Miller

1
4
5
f
mp
f
mp
3
3
ff
8vb

Dialogue

Carolyn Miller

mf
f

English Dance

Carolyn Miller

Allegro moderato

1
D.C al
Coda

Coda
f
mp
cresc. poco a poco
f

F Major Waltz

Andante cantabile

Carolyn Miller

mp
mf
f

R.H. melody
L. H. melody
8va
5
5
mf
mp
8va
p
dim. e poco rit.

G Major March

Moderato

Carolyn Miller

f
mp
f

A Pleasant Day

Carolyn Miller

8va
f
8vb
mf
mp
p
R.H.
L.H.
rit.
8va
L.H.

Beside the Sea

Andante cantabile

R.H. 8va on repeat.

Carolyn Miller